AN EARLY VICTORIAN STREET THE HIGH STREET, OLD PORTSMOUTH

By John Webb, MA, FRHistS

The visitor to Portsmouth who seeks out the original medieval settlement from which the modern city has grown finds at the harbour mouth a distinct, self-contained community, clearly defined and even now set apart from the rest of the island by the line of its former walls. Although the construction of the massive power-station has meant the obliteration of a thousand and more years of history in one sizeable and significant area, much of the town's ancient layout has been retained and the broad, slightly curving High Street is still the main thoroughfare. Devastated by air raids during the Second World War, it has for the most part been rebuilt to provide houses and flats. Only an occasional shop intrudes. Here and there, sometimes pleasantly grouped, Georgian buildings remain to provide a direct link with the town's naval and commercial heyday. Except for the busy Camber area, Old Portsmouth, with its remarkable associations and few remaining historical buildings is, in the last quarter of the twentieth century, essentially a quiet residential backwater and tourist attraction.

In 1837, when Queen Victoria came to the throne, the High Street presented a very different appearance. Then, despite the steady, inexorable development of Portsea, Landport and Southsea, the old town was still the hub of local affairs, and its main street one of the most famous shopping centres in the country. The compiler of *The New Portsmouth Guide*, published in 1839, did not have to exaggerate when he described the 'very handsome street which extends the whole length of the town (about half a mile), adorned with many excellent shops: indeed,' he added proudly, 'its general appearance may rank it among the finest streets out of London.' Other writers shared his opinion. 'We were surprised at the splendour of the shops in High Street,' reported one impartial observer, Thomas Roscoe, a year or two later after a tour of the Isle of Wight, 'as well as the extent and beauty of the street itself.'[1] Charpentier's sixpenny *Stranger's Guide*, published in 1842, provided the early Victorian visitor with a meticulously drawn panorama of this elegant and fashionable shopping centre. Each house and shop was shown in detail, and the names and trades were given of those business and professional people who had subscribed to Mr Charpentier's venture.

Looked at today, the street in the drawing is immensely impressive. The long, almost uninterrupted rows of Georgian façades on each side of the thoroughfare speak eloquently of the wealth which had been brought to the town by the wars in the late eighteenth and early nineteenth centuries. Within a short space of time the investment in bricks and mortar had transformed the old-fashioned town centre into one that was the height of modernity. Mottley, in 1801, described the High Street buildings as 'having been within these few years either rebuilt or new-fronted',[2] and the still comparatively young Henry Slight, writing nearly twenty years later, added a personal note to his comment that the town possessed few old buildings. 'Even in my time,' he wrote, 'most of the low gable-roofed houses of the High Street have given place to the more elegant and convenient edifices of modern architecture.'[3]

In Slight's day Portsmouth was still encircled by massive walls and moats, and access to the town was gained through one or other of the impressive gateways which, much to the annoyance of residents, were closed at midnight by the military. The principal entrance was the Landport Gate which, although today shorn of much of its earlier grandeur, still stands in splendid isolation on its original site. From here, the gently curving upper section of the High Street was reached by following the line of the wall south-eastwards for a short distance along High Street Road (St George's Road) as far as the Town Mount Bastion, now the site of Cambridge Junction.

This end of High Street, down almost as far as the Peacock Lane – Highbury Street crossing, was different in character from the remaining stretch. Here, for the greater part of the early Victorian period, there were no shops. Instead, on both sides, the buildings were mainly private dwellings. Some, the homes of affluent middle–class families, were quite substantial. Number nine, for example, which was described in 1836 as a 'good roomy house', had a parlour, breakfast-room, drawing-room, kitchen, two cellars and six bedrooms, with a stable and coach-house close by.[4] Among those who occupied houses in this part of the High Street during the early years of Queen Victoria were John Spice Hulbert (no. 3), who also had a country house at Purbrook, and Edward Carter (no. 18), a member of one of the most politically active families in the Portsmouth area. Several doctors, solicitors and other professional men also had their homes here, including Thomas Ellis Owen, the architect (no. 16). A few of the dwellings in this part of the street have survived intact, including some from a group of fair-sized town cottages which stood on the right-hand side as the visitor walked towards the sea. Located in this essentially residential, non-commercial part of the High Street were also the handsome Unitarian Chapel and, next door, where Shakespeare Terrace now stands, Mr Way's livery stable, which was sold in 1844 to Mr Owen of Portsmouth Point for £720. Certainly not the most attractive, but undoubtedly the most famous building in this part of town was the Theatre Royal, immortalized by Dickens in *Nicholas Nickleby*, where most of the great actors and actresses of the day appeared at least once during these years. Situated a little above Buckingham House, which was then used partly as a day and boarding school for young ladies, it had behind it, with entrances into both High Street and Penny Street, the Cambridge Barracks. In the early 1850's the whole upper end of this side of the street was bought by the War Office, so that the barracks could be extended. The theatre and the fashionable Georgian houses were demolished and replaced by the bleak but powerful yellow brick building with its stone-framed arched entrance that is now Portsmouth Grammar School.

Below Peacock Lane there were very few private residences, and by the time the market area near the church was reached, both sides of the High Street were lined with shops, with only an occasional bank, hostelry or official building to add variety. The Lieutenant-Governor's residence (between nos. 111 and 112) and the Vicarage (no. 33) were the two most prominent houses in this part of the town. The parish church was almost completely obscured by the High Street buildings situated in front of it, hemming in the ancient and heavily congested churchyard, access to which was gained by the narrow Church Lane, which ran down the side of the Three Tuns, one of the few remaining gabled houses.[5] Until the reign of William IV, the market area hereabouts was dominated by the old 'town house' or guildhall, which stood in the centre of the highway obstructing traffic, but by the time of Queen Victoria's coronation it had been demolished and replaced, on a site next to the Dolphin, by an up-to-date civic and commercial centre, which remained a prominent feature of the street, latterly as the town museum, until the Second World War air raids reduced it to a ruin. The ancient street market was at the same time removed to the section of Penny Street between Pembroke Road and Grand Parade, although at the request of the stallholders trading was allowed in the High Street, between Lombard Street and Oyster Street, during the morning hours on market days (Tuesday, Thursday and Saturday), so long as the highway remained open to vehicular traffic.[6] At its lower end, the High Street came face to face again with the fortifications and curved round to terminate at King James's Gate, beyond which, renamed Broad

Street, it continued as the main thoroughfare of the notorious suburb known as Portsmouth Point.

In 1841 the population of Portsmouth was 9354, of whom almost a thousand (excluding the soldiers and their dependants in Cambridge Barracks) lived in the High Street.[7] Most of these residents occupied the whole of their dwellings, but the street also contained some rented lock-up shops, the upper storeys of which were let separately as private lodgings or, in many cases, as the consulting rooms or offices of doctors, dentists, opticians, solicitors and even (at no. 50) a chiropodist. An advertisement for the auction sale in London in 1845 of number 108, 'a very spacious residence, with conspicuous shop and warehouse, and numerous bedchambers and sitting-rooms', described it as 'applicable for a family hotel or boarding-house'. In fact it remained unoccupied for two years before Sidney Smith and Co. took it over and made it into the Portsmouth Hall of Commerce. Rentals were comparatively low, even by early Victorian standards. Mr Megginson the chemist paid £58 a year in 1847 for the shop and dwelling-house he occupied (no. 113), while at number 75 the shop and warehouse at the rear annually brought in £42 and the private residence £55, the landlord paying rates and taxes in both instances. Although each house was architecturally distinct from its neighbours, the general arrangement was fairly standardized. A good example is the shop of the wine merchant Mr Sayer (no. 48), which in October 1836 was advertised for sale and described in detail. Like most of the High Street buildings it had excellent cellar space, affording Mr Sayer the opportunity to store two thousand dozen bottles. On the ground floor were an entrance hall, counting-house, spirit store and scullery, while the first floor had a drawing-room-cum-library (forty feet by fifteen feet), with folding doors to divide it, a dining-room (twenty-one feet by fourteen feet), a kitchen and two pantries. The two principal bedrooms, with dressing-rooms, together with two servants' bedrooms and an extensive laundry, were on the second floor, and above were two more bedrooms with cupboards. Behind the shop, in Penny Street, was a large three-storeyed building (ninety feet by thirty feet), which had been used for many years as a wholesale candle and soap manufactory. Outhouses and workshops of one kind or another were a common feature at the rear of many of the High Street establishments, and they seem frequently to have had an entrance into a neighbouring road or lane.

The massive sea-walls which overshadowed the

High Street, Portsmouth

lower end of the High Street were the scene of several important changes during this period. The removal in 1848 of the outmoded semaphore which crowned the Square Tower and had for some years been a notable landmark was part of a plan to improve the fortifications on Point. Close by, the new Victoria Pier replaced the old Beef Stage in the early 'forties and quickly became established as a regular calling place for the many steam vessels which served the town. Further along, at the end of Point, the floating bridge began in 1840 to operate an improved ferry service with Gosport. Not only foot passengers but also carriages, carts and the substantial military traffic could now cross the harbour in comfort and with little difficulty, thus avoiding the irksome journey round by road. In the early days of the floating bridge project, there was talk of making Portsea Hard the terminus, but the apathy of the traders in that area and strong pressure from within Portsmouth resulted in the slightly shorter route. Many of the High Street traders, realising the significance of the proposed

service, became shareholders in the venture, and it is worth noting that the case that was made for the floating bridge in 1838 included the prediction that there would be an influx of shoppers from Gosport into Portsmouth, 'because they can buy goods of every description much cheaper, of a better quality, and may have a better selection than they get at Gosport'.[8] In these years, too, attempts were made to improve the wharfs and docks of the Camber by a development scheme initiated by the Corporation.

The streets of Portsmouth had been paved since the 1770's, and a body of Improvement Commissioners, set up by Act of Parliament, met from time to time, often reluctantly, to deal with matters concerning their physical appearance and maintenance. These men ordered the streets to be macadamised, appointed scavengers who organised rubbish disposal, arranged for the drains and gutters to be flushed and public wells and pumps kept in order, saw to the removal of nuisances and obstructions in the streets, and regulated the parking of carts and carriages. In the

1820's they installed gas lighting in place of the old oil lamps. Despite the Commissioners' efforts, the unhygienic condition of the town and the high incidence of disease were matters of frequent public debate. 'There are few towns in England, Sir, which are thus neglected,' wrote 'M.D.' to the editor of the *Hampshire Telegraph* in September 1841. 'The drains are not covered as in most towns, nor cleansed by a running stream as in Salisbury, but are in a foul and stagnant condition. . .' In October 1848 another correspondent drew attention to 'the dirty and unhealthy state' of the streets, especially those near the Camber. 'At the moment.' he concluded, 'the stench is dreadful from the decaying vegetable and animal deposit upon the surface of these streets and the heaps of putrid matter in the centre.' The system of moats, infrequently flushed and neglected by the military authorities, had become an unofficial rubbish tip and common sewer, and the noisome stagnant waters were a source of great offence to the inhabitants, especially during the summer months.

The High Street was probably much cleaner than many of the town's thoroughfares, particularly after the removal elsewhere of the greater part of the street market trade. The shopkeepers and private residents in their comfortable, well-appointed establishments were much less a prey to disease than the ill-fed inhabitants of the squalid courts and alleys with their polluted water supply only a stone's throw away. Significantly, the High Street was little affected by the great cholera outbreak of 1848-49, only two isolated cases being reported there according to the Rawlinson *Report* (1850). Elsewhere in the town scores died. At the height of the epidemic the victims were hastily buried in batches at first light in the already seriously congested churchyard of St Thomas's.

When he wrote an account of Portsmouth in his *Hampshire*, published in 1838, Robert Mudie noted that 'some of the inns and hotels are on a scale of considerable magnitude; but,' he went on, 'none of them has any very strong claims to attention, especially in a town where there are so many matters worthier of notice.' In the High Street there were six establishments which provided the local inhabitants with centres of social activity and the many visitors with refreshment and lodging. Adjoining the new market house was the Dolphin which when it was sold by auction in 1840 was described as a 'well accustomed, highly respectable freehold inn and tavern . . . most

advantageously situated'. Higher up the street on the same side, where now stands George Court, was the George Hotel, which was run by the Guy family during the early years of the reign. An imposing building with a substantial frontage, including the characteristic arched entrance of the typical coaching inn, it was rivalled in importance only by the Fountain, which stood almost opposite Oyster Street. Mottley, in 1801, gave a vivid description of this latter hostelry which he claimed had accommodation for 170 guests and a dining-room which could seat 200. 'And such is the constant influx of company here,' he concluded, 'that a laundress has a house upon the premises, where she solely employs herself and several other women in washing the linen of the customers.' Mottley was writing during the hotel's heyday, but at the accession of Queen Victoria it continued to be a fashionable resort. On the corner of Grand Parade, on a site now occupied by Fontenoy House, was the old-established business best known as 'Neale's', or the Grand Parade Hotel, although it operated during this period under several different names. Henry Slight recalled: 'The Parade Coffee-house and Hotel . . . was formerly the house of the Captains of the Navy, and in the "olden time" . . . it was not uncommon to see . . . (them) sitting outside this house on forms, smoking long pipes.'[9] On this side of the street too, a few steps from the Square Tower, stood the Wellington. Until his death in 1843, aged seventy, this inn was run by Mr Kiln, who was a local worthy well known to the writer George Meredith, who had been born and brought up in his family's naval outfitter's shop opposite, and introduced him into his novel *Evan Harrington*.[10] Although Kiln's widow attempted to carry on the business and advertised 'Good accommodation for travellers, with well-aired beds', she had been forced within a few months to hand over the tenancy to George Knight of the Three Horseshoes. Finally, on the other side of the street, on the corner of Church Lane, was the Three Tuns, the landlord of which was Thomas Parkinson. During the Spithead Mutiny this inn had been a meeting-place of the sailors' delegates. There Lord Howe and his fellow officers had been obliged to wait on the stairs while the mutineers completed their deliberations.[11] The Crown, one of the most famous hotels in Portsmouth during the Napoleonic Wars, was not functioning at this period. Instead the buildings had been divided up into shops, showrooms and lodging houses (nos. 34-36).

The High Street hostelries were the centres of considerable social activity during the course of a year. The pages of the *Hampshire Telegraph* record innumerable dinners, concerts, gatherings of clubs and societies, and official business meetings of local companies. A constant stream of visitors found accommodation even in peace-time, and the George and the Fountain were patronised by a very distinguished *clientèle*. Princes and peers, generals and gentry passed regularly through their doors. The guest list at the George for a week in May 1839 is by no means exceptional. It included Prince Edward of Saxe-Weimar, Lord Adolphus FitzClarence, the Earl of Dundonald, Viscount Exmouth, Viscount Ingestrie, Lord Henry Clinton, Lord and Lady Francis Egerton, and others of lesser but still considerable standing. A few weeks later there arrived from Buckingham Palace Duke Ferdinand of Saxe-Coburgh, Princess Victoire, Prince Augustus and Prince Leopold of Saxe-Coburgh, the Prince of Leiningen, Count Alexander Mensdorf and Baroness Fenyevessey.

One of the best known sounds in the High Street at this period must have been the clatter of the stage-coaches as they left with their passengers from the various picking-up points. Over the years the times and details of the service changed, but an indication of the busy coach traffic may be gained from an examination of the 1839 *Portsmouth Guide*. The principal route was to London, although Brighton, Bristol, Chichester, Oxford and Winchester were also served. The coach offices at 61 High Street, the George, the Fountain, the Globe in Oyster Street and the Blue Posts in Broad Street saw regular departures, mainly at half-hourly intervals during the weekday mornings, of coaches with such stirring names as the Tantivy, Star of Brunswick, Celerity, Defiance, Sovereign, Royal Blue, and Rocket, as well as the Royal Mail. Carriers' carts plied principally from inns in the side streets of the old town.

Unfortunately for Andrew Nance, Thomas Parkinson and the other coach proprietors, a revolution in transport was in progress. During the next few years they made every effort to save the situation. As early as June 1838, the so-called Railway Coach began to operate from Bath Square to link up with the London train service from Woking Station. To the amazement of the editor of the *Hampshire Telegraph*, the capital could now be reached from Halfway House in six-and-a-half-hours. As the railway crept towards Portsmouth, this policy of linking the townspeople with the nearest train service developed. By 1842 Gosport Station had opened and offered a direct route to the capital, and Nance and Parkinson were providing omnibus services to and

from the harbour ferry for passengers and their baggage.

Across the street from the George stood the Lieutenant-Governor's house, an imposing residence which, until a few years earlier, had been the official home of the Port Admiral. Henry Slight told how, 'since the occupancy of General MacMahon it has undergone much improvement and repair. The garden behind is extensive, and the stabling and offices are in St Thomas's Street.'[12] The interior of the house must have been revealed to few of the local residents, but a glimpse was provided in 1847 when MacMahon's successor, Sir Hercules Pakenham, sold by auction many of the contents. Two fine ormolu chandeliers, one with twenty lights and the other with fifteen, Albert sofas, tête-à-tête seats, figured damask and crimson moreen window curtains, and lofty mahogany and birch four-posters with chinz hangings and window curtains to match, came under the auctioneer's hammer, as did many more mundane items, such as blinds, fenders, a patent mangle, flower stands, a cucumber frame, 700 greenhouse plants, and a 'handsome half-bred Norman cow', together with a cowhouse.

But if the interior of this grand mansion was seen by few, the sentry who paraded outside was obvious to many and the source of general annoyance. One Tuesday afternoon late in 1839 matters came to a head. George Holloway, a horseman, was standing on the pavement outside the Lieutenant-Governor's residence awaiting the arrival of the Regulator coach, 'as was his custom and his duty to do'. While there, the sentry, Patrick Flanders, ordered him to move on. When the horseman refused, an argument ensured, during which Flanders threatened him with his musket and bayonet, 'and desired him to go into the sentry-box, which Holloway refused to do'. When a servant came to the door, presumably on the orders of a superior, and spoke to him, the sentry calmed down, and Holloway angrily made off to complain to the police. The *Hampshire Telegraph*, quick to react, asked its readers, 'What possible right has a sentry, or any military man, to determine the privileges of civilians in the public streets?' The following week the editor, returning to the matter, described the sentry as a public nuisance. That very afternoon, 'he was parading . . . in front of Sir Hercules Pakenham's railing, in the centre of a pavement not seven feet wide, to the discomforture of any two gentlemen, or any two ladies that may be passing up street. As we said last week, if this military puppet must be kept for show, he should be directed

to parade inside the railing, or within the general's capacious porch; but in no wise ought he to be allowed to annoy or interfere with the civilians in passing up and down the most public street of the town.'

Many of the civilians so offended must have been townsfolk and visitors intent on making their purchases in the High Street shops. From the wide variety of clothing on display they could acquire such items as silk Tuscan and Dunstable bonnets, Foster's patent parama waterproof clothing, and the New Universal Paletot, 'now so generally worn by ladies of fashion . . . an article of dress combining extreme gentility with unequalled comfort, the nature of the material promoting a healthy circulation and a genial warmth throughout the whole system, and preventing the injurious action of damp and foggy weather upon ladies of delicate constitution'. Marie Stuart walking cloaks, 'the favourite shape in Paris', and similar French fashions were brought back regularly from the continent by Miss Mayell and her fellow dress-shop owners. Footwear included styles 'as worn and patronised by Prince Albert', impilia boots, and French shoes, the superior elegance and exquisite comfort of which, it was maintained by Mr McCartney (no. 104), 'makes all comment superfluous to the fashionables to whom this announcement is made'. At Mr Sheppard's (no. 55) could be had his own make of 'patent india rubber, lined, wash deck, sporting and walking shoes and boots, which he can warrant effectually to resist the damp; and . . . buckskin, dogskin, and all kinds of boots and shoes shall be got up in accordance with the prevailing fashions'. This shop later became a pork butcher's, its owner, Joseph Adnams, also dealing in oysters, which he was willing to serve his patrons in his 'respectable

oyster rooms', or dispatch in barrels to any part of the kingdom. Another delicacy could be obtained a few doors down the street at a grocer's store (no. 58), now part of the Sallyport Hotel. This was 'the great staple food of the E. Indies, the curry, hitherto so little known in this country . . . perfect as it is used in Bengal, accompanied by instructions for its application in general cookery'. Across the street, a few doors from the Three Tuns, was in 1846 Mr Fraser's confectionery shop (no. 91). As a sideline he carried on in summer a seasonal trade in ice-creams and water-ices, with Wenham Lake ice always available and 'sent any distance with little waste'; in winter he turned to soupmaking and 'packed and sent' his wares 'to any part'. In 1846 'a fine lively turtle' which was killed at the Fountain and 'dressed by a London cook', produced soup which was sold at five shillings a quart. At Mr Chamney's shop (no. 37) could be bought pastries and pies, and digestive and fancy bread, 'ready for shipment or household use'. In 1848 the *Hampshire Telegraph* complained that most of the bakers in the borough sold bread underweight, and 'such a thing as best bread is unknown . . . No baker buys better flour than the best seconds.' Many beverages could be obtained, including Bass and Allsop's East India pale ales, Schweppes's soda water, and a wide range of locally manufactured soft drinks. Other goods available included Sheffield plated articles, musical boxes, and lava ornaments from Vesuvius and Etna which could be purchased in 1843 at 75 High Street while customers heard 'an elegant self-playing euterpeon performing some of the finest airs of the new operas', and the 'three very elegant chandeliers, worth inspection, one of which is believed to have belonged to the Emperor

The lower part of the High Street, probably about 1840. The Wellington tavern is on the immediate right. George Meredith was born opposite in the shop with slender pillars and first floor bay window (no. 73). The Guildhall can be seen in the distance.

Napoleon', and the 'elegant rosewood circular chess table, top inlaid with ivory', which could be obtained at Mr Fiske's (no. 59). On sale in 1848 at number 102 was the so-called 'Baby Jumper, or Patent Elastic Infant Gymnasium'. This unusual invention cost from ten to twenty-five shillings, according to style, and was a means 'by which children of three months of age and upwards can exercise and amuse themselves. It combines ease with health, and ensures the delight of the child with the repose of the mother.' Next door, at Emanuel's (no. 101), there were, besides the displays of silverware, clocks, watches, jewellery, and Braham's superior patent pantoscopic spectacles, many articles made from the timbers of the *Royal George*. One of the choicest items, an elegant octagonal table supported by four carved lions, was sent by the loyal Emanuel brothers, together with a model of the ill-fated ship, to the Queen at Windsor.

Mr Emanuel Emanuel, goldsmith to the Queen, was only one of several High Street shopkeepers who had had royal patronage conferred on them. The street panorama of 1842 refers to Mr Sayer (no. 48) as 'wine merchant to Her Majesty', and elsewhere Mr Davis (no. 116) was described as music seller to the royal family, Mr Hay (no. 53) as her and her mother's operative chemist, and Mr Chamney (no. 37) as royal fancy bread and biscuit baker. Also claiming royal patronage at this time was George Stebbing, whose shop (no. 66) was near the Square Tower. In his advertisements he referred to himself as 'optician by appointment to Her Majesty, H.R.H. the Duchess of Kent, and the R.Y.S.'. He also claimed to be 'upwards of thirty years compass maker to the Royal Navy . . . (and maker of) bittacles, in wood and brass, plain and ornamental, with his improved mode of lighting now used in Her Majesty's Navy, introduced in 1821, for which, and his improving the compass, he received from the Hon. Navy Board one hundred pounds'. Much to his annoyance his eldest son, also an optician and instrument maker, opened a rival shop in Broad Street. George junior is of particular interest because a few years earlier he had been instrument maker on board H.M. sloop *Beagle* during the epic circumnavigation when Darwin had developed his theory of evolution.

When George Stebbing senior gave up business in 1847 he had been established in the High Street since the beginning of the century. Thomas Sheppard, the boot and shoe maker, had set up even earlier, in the year of the Spithead mutiny. Several of the shops had passed through the hands of more than one generation.

The Diapers, father and son, completed almost half a century of trading when 83 High Street was taken over by W. G. Chambers in 1844, and the Merediths (no. 73) had been providing uniforms for naval and military officers since the 1780's when the Great Mel's old business failed through his son's deficiencies in the 1830's. Even longer in trade was the Clarke family, whose ironmongery shop was a feature of the Portsmouth scene for almost a century until its sale in 1839. It would be wrong, however, to see the High Street as consisting largely of old-established family businesses with few opportunities for new men to set up shop. There was considerable mobility, probably increased during the early years of the Queen's reign by the unpropitious economic climate. Tradesmen moved from one part of the street to another; shop-keepers came and went; seemingly flourishing firms went bankrupt almost overnight.

One such collapse was that of T. H. Fiske, the ironmonger. In 1839 he took over Clarke's business at 82 High Street and confidently boasted: 'In the extensive manufacturing branches experienced work-men only will be employed, and particular attention paid to orders for stoves, kitchen ranges, and cooking apparatus of every description, bell-hanging, ship's and yacht's fittings, guns, smith's work, etc., naval and military messes, and every department of fur-nishing and general ironmongery; consequently a prompt and satisfactory execution of all orders may be relied on. . .' The business apparently thrived during the next few years. In November 1846 all seemed to be going well. Fiske gave his workmen their annual supper at the Wellington, and 'the evening was spent in great harmony and conviviality.' Alas! discord was soon to follow. By mid-February Fiske had been declared bankrupt and his property was put up for sale.

More spectacular was the disaster which befell Burbey, Loe and Co. (no. 46) in 1841. Thomas Burbey, who was uncle by marriage to George Meredith, and had been for some years a leading figure in the town, was a partner in business with Richard and James Loe. As bankers, merchants and dealers their interests were complex. At a meeting of their creditors held at the George in December 1841, it was said that excluding mortgages they owed £20,000. They themselves were owed nearly £15,000 by their cus-tomers, but 'bad debts' accounted for £11,000, and a further £500 was described as 'doubtful.' Their private properties were calculated as likely to produce £4,000. During the days before Christmas the bank-rupts' assets were realised. Mahogany counters,

9

copper scales, sets of brass weights, tea canisters, a cask of York hams, a powerful cart-horse, two broad-wheel carts, and many other items fell beneath the auctioneer's hammer at 46 High Street, together with the partners' household furniture, 'applicable to the various departments of a genteel residence'. Silver plate, linen, richly cut decanters, ten dozen claret, two hogsheads of home-made wine, a rosewood drawing-room suite, four-poster beds, and 2,000 volumes of classics, history and divinity were trundled off unceremoniously. A few months later, to complete the partners' private tragedy, a meadow and various investment properties in Gloucester Place were sold off. Of the workpeople who suffered loss of employment as a result of their masters' misfortunes we hear nothing.

During the early Victorian period, a considerable number of men, women and young people found employment in the High Street. They included craftsmen, coachmen, labourers, shop assistants, apprentices and, above all, domestic servants, most of whom lived at their places of work. The census returns give detailed information about the resident servant population. In 1841, 30 men and 204 women were put in this category by the High Street enumerators. Ten years later, the numbers had altered little: 37 men and 196 women. Thus almost one-quarter of the street's total population consisted of servants, and this explains the significantly high proportion of women to men over-all. Most of these were domestics of one kind or another. In 1841, for example, Edward Carter had four female servants, aged 65, 30, 22 and 15 years, and a male servant aged 34. At Government House in 1851, Lord Frederick Fitzclarence's family was served by four lady's maids, a housekeeper, a butler, a cook, two house-maids, two kitchenmaids, a stillroom maid, a footman, a postillion, a groom, and an undefined general servant. Some indication of the wages paid can be obtained from an advertisement which W. G. Chambers placed in the *Hampshire Telegraph* in 1847. He wanted to employ a woman aged thirty to forty years to look after four children. His was 'a family where a man and another woman are kept', and he offered wages of £10 a year, 'to be increased after the first year if found suitable'.

In 1841 there were twelve apprentices living in their master's houses. Two each were training to be surgeons, pastry-cooks, chemists and booksellers, and one each as a confectioner, a tailor, a silversmith and an engraver. Their ages ranged from twelve to twenty-one. Advertisements for apprentices were commonplace in the local newspaper. In 1847 the *Hampshire Telegraph* itself needed a boy. He had to be 'an intelligent lad, grounded in the Latin classics, and with a knowledge of French would be preferred; and if steady, would in his progress through life, be sure to do well'. Usually a premium was required, and this, it is clear from an example in 1844, could be quite substantial. In that year, J. E. Vardy the draper (no. 108) went into voluntary liquidation. His apprentice, Richard Henry Rogers, applied for the return of a portion of the premium of £99 which had been paid on his behalf in May 1841, apparently for a five-year term. Vardy vigorously opposed the claim, 'as the youth was worth £20 a year, and his food and lodging, to any person in the trade'. The matter was adjourned to enable a new master to be found, it being emphasised that 'care should be taken that whatever money the court might award should be applied for the benefit of the apprentice'.

Shop assistants, both male and female, were among the most hard-pressed members of the High Street community. That they had to be of some quality is illustrated by an advertisement inserted in the *Hampshire Telegraph* in March 1838 by C. & C. Coles, whose drapery establishment, London House (no. 78), was opposite Grand Parade. 'A young man of respectable connections and indisputable character for honesty, sobriety, and experience, that can bear inscrutability', was required, and it was emphasised that 'none need apply but will answer the above description: a Dissenter will be preferred'. High standards were still being maintained nine years later, when the same firm sought 'a respectable young man with unexceptionable references'. Shop assistants felt a sense of superiority over their fellow workers, and were sustained by a vague hope, rarely realised, that they themselves would one day rise into the employing class. In reality they were among the most downtrodden of all early Victorian workers. Mostly young men and women under the age of thirty-five, they frequently lived in cramped conditions on the premises and had to accept their employer's word as law.[13]

At the root of their problem was the inordinately long working day. Both male and female assistants were required to remain standing for many hours, during which they were often allowed to snatch only a few minutes' respite for meals. For six days each

week they toiled from early morning until late at night, so that on the seventh those who had the will to go to church invariably slumbered in their pews. 'The tainted atmosphere, the scanty exercise, the irregular hours, the long confinement, the uniform position, all contribute to deteriorate the health, and aggravate the depressing influence of the life passed behind the counter', a local observer commented in 1847. Not for them was there the opportunity open to most of their fellow workers to engage in invigorating outdoor pursuits. 'The fine, healthy, manly sports of winter and summer, the skating of the former and the cricket of the latter are denied to the young men who stand fourteen or fifteen hours daily behind the counter.' The extent of their deterioration was summarised by a clergyman, the Rev. Charles Room. 'It cannot but be obvious to those who have paid the slightest attention to the method in which business is now carried on in our shops,' he told a Portsmouth audience, 'that it is utterly impossible for the assistants of tradesmen to pay an adequate attention to their domestic, social, moral and religious duties.'

During the first years of Victoria's reign, at a time when there was increasing agitation for reforms of all kinds, attempts were made in some of the larger towns to form organisations which would press for an improvement in shopworkers' conditions. In Portsmouth attention was first focussed on the problem in September 1843, when a letter from an anonymous correspondent was printed in the *Hampshire Telegraph*. 'Is it just,' the writer asked, 'that a class of respectable and deserving young men should be deprived of the time so necessary for air and exercise – to say nothing of improvement – that is enjoyed by mechanics of every grade, because those who wish to purchase goods procrastinate the time for doing so to an unreasonably late hour in the evening?'

The *Hampshire Telegraph*, ever-ready to espouse a good cause, commented on the matter in an editorial a week or two later. It noted with pleasure that 'several influential gentlemen' had taken up the shopworkers' cause, and reminded its readers of their vital contribution to the debate. 'It is not so much a question to be settled between the employers and employed . . . the irresistible voice of public opinion must say yea or nay to the continuance of a system so prejudicial to health and morality.' A fortnight later the newspaper reported that at the request of 120 inhabitants the mayor had convened a public meeting to consider curtailing hours of business. 'As there will be much

11

diversity of opinion as to the hours at which the shops should generally close,' wrote the editor, 'we would beg to offer the following arrangement: from November 15 to February 14, seven o'clock; from February 15 to May 14, eight o'clock; from May 15 to August 14, nine o'clock; from August 15 to November 14, eight o'clock.' Nothing was said about times of opening. These hours, which still seem extremely long to us, were advanced by the newspaper as a great improvement on the existing situation. The scheme, it was maintained, 'will give about 360 hours less labour, and we trust consequently so many hours of what we may hope usefully expended time'.

Late in October 1843, 'a very numerous and highly respectable meeting of the inhabitants' took place at the Beneficial Hall under the chairmanship of the mayor. Among the speakers was Dr Meadows, who drew attention particularly to the linen drapers and told his audience: 'Their pallid cheek, produced by the little opportunity they had of refreshing their body, and having to snatch their hasty meals, betoken the inroads made on their health. Their labours were needlessly long, and hard beyond measure. . . For the reasons he had assigned, many of that class go to a premature grave, and so impressed was he that the whole were predisposed to disease, that he would never certify one of them to be a fit subject for an insurance office.'

The result of such eloquence was the founding of the Borough of Portsmouth Association for Shortening the Hours of Business. Membership was open to all who paid five shillings a year. Under the presidency of the Rev. Dewdney, it recommended nine o'clock closing from 25 March to 29 September, and eight o'clock during the remaining months. Saturday closing was to be ten o'clock throughout the year. To most of the shopkeepers these hours seem to have been acceptable. The shops in Portsea responded immediately, although the *Hampshire Telegraph* reported that not all members benefited equally. 'We are assured . . . by some leading drapers that, as far as their businesses are concerned, themselves and their assistants gain but little, as on the closing of the outer shutters they have their work before them to clear up, which seldom occupies less than an hour and a half.' The newspaper suggested that the drapers should agree among themselves to close at seven o'clock, at least during the three winter months. In Landport some shopkeepers failed to comply with the association's scheme, and in Portsmouth 'the obstinacy of one or two individuals' was said to be

sabotaging the whole plan. 'A deputation from the association has been appointed to wait on these persons,' it was reported, 'and we trust that they will be induced to yield to the wishes of their neighbours.'

During the next three years the attempt to limit hours of business continued, but it was not easy to get the full co-operation of the public. People had long been used to buying wares until a late hour, and shopkeepers were loath to close their doors in their customers' faces. 'Time must be given for the formation of new habits,' wrote the secretary of the association, 'and irregularity and difference borne with till these habits shall have been formed.' Another problem was that although the dockyard and some private establishments paid their workers on Friday, other employers caused unnecessary inconvenience by not doing so until late the following day. The association, 'not unmindful of the objection that if workmen

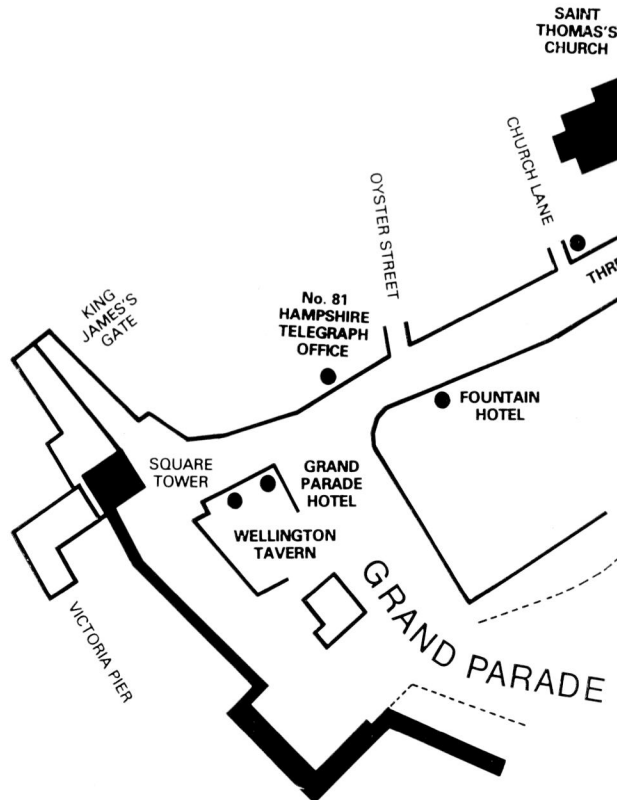

SAINT THOMAS'S CHURCH

CHURCH LANE

OYSTER STREET

THREE

No. 81 HAMPSHIRE TELEGRAPH OFFICE

FOUNTAIN HOTEL

KING JAMES'S GATE

SQUARE TOWER

GRAND PARADE HOTEL

WELLINGTON TAVERN

VICTORIA PIER

GRAND PARADE

Portsmouth High Street about 1840

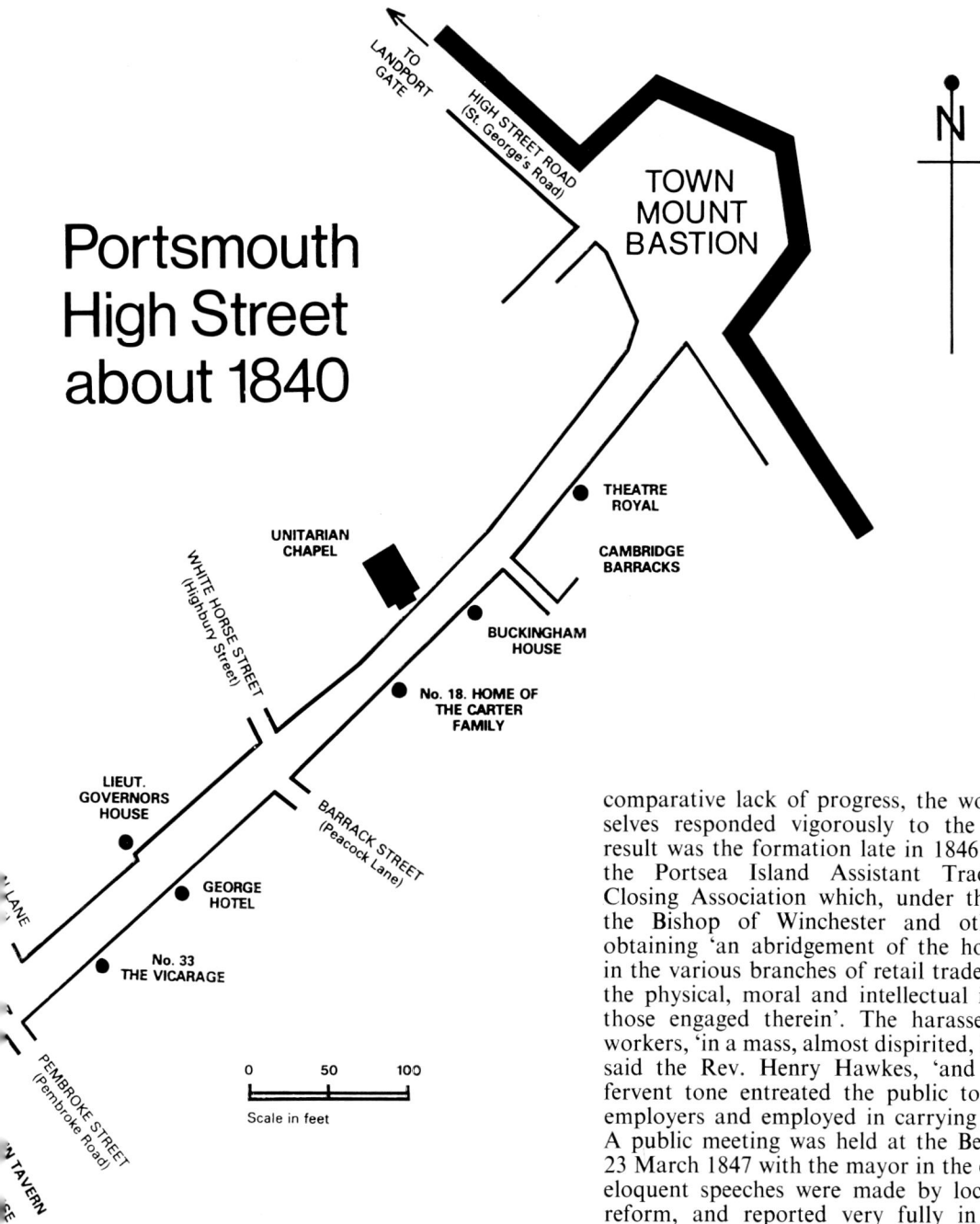

TO LANDPORT GATE

HIGH STREET ROAD (St. George's Road)

TOWN MOUNT BASTION

N

THEATRE ROYAL

CAMBRIDGE BARRACKS

UNITARIAN CHAPEL

BUCKINGHAM HOUSE

WHITE HORSE STREET (Highbury Street)

No. 18. HOME OF THE CARTER FAMILY

LIEUT. GOVERNORS HOUSE

BARRACK STREET (Peacock Lane)

GEORGE HOTEL

No. 33 THE VICARAGE

LANE

PEMBROKE STREET (Pembroke Road)

N TAVERN SE

0   50   100

Scale in feet

comparative lack of progress, the workpeople themselves responded vigorously to the challenge. The result was the formation late in 1846 of a new body, the Portsea Island Assistant Tradesmen's Early Closing Association which, under the patronage of the Bishop of Winchester and others, aimed at obtaining 'an abridgement of the hours of business in the various branches of retail trade, with a view to the physical, moral and intellectual improvement of those engaged therein'. The harassed young shopworkers, 'in a mass, almost dispirited, had now arisen,' said the Rev. Henry Hawkes, 'and with deep and fervent tone entreated the public to work with the employers and employed in carrying out the object'. A public meeting was held at the Beneficial Hall on 23 March 1847 with the mayor in the chair, and many eloquent speeches were made by local advocates of reform, and reported very fully in the *Hampshire Telegraph*. The presence of Charles Nash, the secretary of the Metropolitan Early Closing Association, indicates that the sponsors of the new organisation were well aware of the need for moral support and advice from outside Portsea Island.

Of particular interest is the speech of Mr Groves, a High Street butcher (no. 38) who was strongly in favour of the assistants' cause. He said:

'As a tradesman himself he should like to have an hour in the evening in his own family. (Hear, hear.) Let it be remembered that it was not only young men who were confined twelve or fourteen hours daily behind the counter, but young women also . . . it was bad enough for men to be worked so long, but it was a disgrace for females to be exposed to it. (Hear, hear.) There was an

be paid on a Friday they will waste the Saturday in idleness and dissipation', pressed for general payment on the earlier day.

Although most shopkeepers were sympathetic to their employees' cause, since they themselves benefited from reduced working hours and smaller gas bills and appreciated that an educated public would do the same amount of shopping in less time, there were some who were openly hostile and broke the agreement, so that their neighbours felt bound to follow suit to avoid loss of custom. Frustrated by the employer in the borough whose name he would not mention, who was an enemy to closing early; the assistants in his shop wished to have the advantage of attending the meeting, and certain young men waited on him to request that they might be allowed to do so. His reply was, "Oh no, we have other fish to fry; I shall keep my shop open till nine o'clock tonight!" (Cries of "shame, shame", and "name him.")... Ladies should not buy by the delusive glare of gas light . . . they should make their purchases by daylight. If they were determined that "Britain never should have slaves", they would never come to a shop after dark. Let all the shopkeepers too in Portsmouth, Portsea, Landport, and Southsea, be determined to put an end to it – Landport in particular. (Hear, hear.) He hoped that Landport instead of being behind would be forward in this movement. (Cheers.)'

Five resolutions, 'prepared by the young men themselves', were unanimously adopted. They reaffirmed the need for all shopworkers to have more leisure time for intellectual and recreational pursuits, and for a curtailment of shop hours. The fourth, proposed by Mr Groves, called for seven o'clock closing in the evening during the winter months and eight o'clock during the summer. These hours would 'in no way compromise the interests of the employers, or in the least degree inconvenience the public'. The struggle for better working conditions continued over the horizon of the early Victorian period. If *The History of Mr Polly* and *Kipps* are a true reflection of H. G. Wells's experiences in the world of the drapery store, there had been few improvements by the early 1880's when he became an assistant at Hyde's of Southsea. Even the indefatigable Father Dolling had little success a year or two later when he attempted to organise the shopworkers and improve their dreary lot.[14]

At last came Sunday. According to the *Hampshire Telegraph* in September 1845, 'the Sabbath is held in these towns in a much more quiet and orderly way than in many others; and indeed, considering the assemblage of seamen, soldiers, and the mass of labourers, of which our population is composed, we are inclined to think it offers in its Sunday's appearance a fit example for many populous places'. No doubt most of the High Street residents attended religious services of one kind or another. The parish church of St Thomas, the interior of which was sketched in 1837 by R. H. C. Ubsdell, a local artist, was by this time totally inadequate. It was said that it held not more than 1400 persons, exclusive of children, 'and consequently that not one-fourth of the parishioners can be accommodated with sittings . . . and that no accommodation is therein provided for

the poor, with the exception of the aisles. . .' In order to relieve the pressure a chapel of ease, St Mary's, was consecrated in August 1839. Designed by Thomas Ellis Owen and providing 1200 sittings, it stood on the north side of the town near Colewort Barracks, on part of the site now occupied by the power-station. The vicar of both Portsmouth and Portsea at the beginning of the reign was the Rev. Charles Henville who in 1827-28 had rebuilt the Vicarage in the High Street (no. 33) at a cost of £2,000. In 1838 he was succeeded by the Rev. John McGhie, whose incumbency lasted until 1868. During his time at St Thomas's the internal appearance of the parish church underwent many changes, including a major programme of repair and reconstruction in 1843, which necessitated the closure of the building to the public from April until August.[15] For the armed forces and some civilians there was the unrestored Garrison Church, the centre of much military splendour and pageantry during the course of the year. The Unitarian Chapel in the High Street also underwent extensive repairs in 1843. There were various other nonconformist meeting places in the side-streets of the town, but Portmuthians seem to have had less denominational choice than their neighbours in Portsea and Landport. Emanuel Emanuel and his fellow Jews, on their sabbath, were served by the synagogue in White's Row, Portsea.

An interesting glimpse of the churchgoing habits of Portsmouth people is afforded by the ecclesiastical census taken on 30 March 1851.[16] Unfortunately no record survives for the parish church, but St Mary's had 518 worshippers in the morning and 516 in the evening. The figures for the Garrison Church were 668 (morning) and 840 (afternoon), and it was noted that although attendance fluctuated according to the state of the garrison it was usually filled twice each Sunday with two different congregations. The chapel of the gaol had 51 at the morning service and 52 at that in the afternoon. The statistics of the Unitarian Chapel were somewhat vague. About 144 were present in the morning and 'rather more' in the evening. Attendance at other places of worship within the ramparts were: Wesleyan Bethel, Bath Square, 94 (morning), 92 (afternoon), 40 (evening); Wesleyan Chapel, Green Row, 537, 96, 458; Highbury Independent Chapel, 267 (morning), 307 (evening); General Baptist Chapel, St Thomas's Street, 43, 19, 35.

During the summer months, if the moats were in a reasonable state of cleanliness, the ramparts provided the townspeople with a pleasant Sunday stroll. In

1849 J. M. W. Turner the artist, visiting Portsmouth on a tour of southern England, spoke of the walls being used by the inhabitants 'as an agreeable lounge and promenade, and afford ever varying views of the shipping and surrounding scenery'. Another observer in 1850 also remarked on the attractiveness of the walk, with its lines of fine elms, and added, 'and when the garrison band is playing on the green in front of the Governor's House, near the King's Bastion, the enlivening scene is only such as can be displayed in a garrison town'. Some years earlier, Henry Alford, writing to his cousin Fanny, had also commented on the contribution music made to the life of the towns-people. 'There are some very good military bands here,' he wrote, 'and they play on the fortifications every night at nine o'clock, till nearly ten. The music is very fine; you can imagine me highly delighted with it.'[17] At times, however, the presence of the soldiery with their various activities could irritate even the most loyal inhabitant. 'We had hoped the disgraceful custom of crying down the credit of a regiment had been discontinued,' wrote the editor of the *Hampshire Telegraph* in August 1842, 'but we regretted much this morning to find the 16th Regiment put it into practice, with all the noise and parade of drums and fifes, opposite our office windows.'

Music was undoubtedly one of the major leisure pursuits of the townspeople. If the poorer inhabitants had little opportunity to do more than listen to the strident tunes of the military bands or join in the shanties and popular songs in the backstreet beer-houses, the better-off gathered in innumerable front parlours to enjoy musical soirées in which they gave voice to more respectable ballads. For a time a favourite Tuesday evening resort was the Dolphin Hotel, where the Portsmouth Philharmonic Society held its concerts. In March 1837 it was reported that the week's meeting had been a great success, 'and the glees, songs, etc. accompanied by that talented pianist, Mr Bell, performed in such a style as to draw forth rapturous applause from a crowded and highly respectable company'. Young ladies with social ambitions were expected to be able to sing prettily and play the piano with some degree of competence. Lessons were available from several talented teachers. In 1847 for example, the versatile J. G. Jones, 'professor of music (bandmaster of the 43rd light infantry)', announced that he was willing to give lessons on the harp, pianoforte, flute, guitar and cornopean. The following year Miss Green, who could be hired to sing and play at evening parties, offered to take pupils to learn Italian and English singing, the piano and elocution. No doubt tuition could also be had from John Balsir Chatterton, a Portmuthian who in 1847 was appointed harpist to the Queen. Early in the reign Mr Davis, 'professor of the Spanish guitar and singing', lived at 116 High Street and combined his teaching with a successful music shop. Further down the street, opposite the parish church, was Mr Hinton's emporium (no. 54) where in 1847

15

a six-and-a-half octave, rosewood cottage pianoforte with pillars could be had for £35, reduced from the maker's price of fifty-five guineas. Also concerned with the sale of sheet music and musical instruments at this period were Z. Slaney (no. 29) and J. Cole (no. 102).

But of all the musical families in the High Street, the foremost place was undoubtedly held by the Treakells. Until the early 'forties they lived at number 63, next door to the Wellington, but then moved their pianoforte manufactory across to number 74, which had once been Admiral Anson's home. Here Mr Treakell and his large and talented family sold musical instruments of every description, and claimed 'not to be surpassed by any house in or out of London'. Lessons were offered on the pianoforte and Spanish guitar. The lower end of High Street must often have been filled with musical sounds as the Treakells practised and taught, and prepared for the various public concerts at which they performed. 'The more frequently we hear Mr and Miss M. A. Treakell's performance on the pianoforte,' a *Hampshire Telegraph* writer commented in 1841, 'the more highly we appreciate it.' The following year Mr Treakell joined forces with Henry Lambeth, the newly appointed organist of the parish church, to instruct some of the boys of the national school in the Hullah system of singing, a 'new system of warble' which was publicly demonstrated at the Green Row Rooms in August 1842. Another member of the Treakell family, Theodore, composed the Osborne Polka, which was played to Queen Victoria by a band of the Royal Marines in 1847. 'Her Majesty was pleased with it,' reported the *Hampshire Telegraph*, 'and her attention was so much aroused as to command its repetition, and after a few bars of the encore, she seized Prince Albert's arm, and polkad on the greensward for some minutes. We confess we are not surprised at this,' it added, 'as we know no reason why royal ears and royal feet should not be pleased and put in action by the same sweet sounds that set common limbs in joyful motion.'

Amateur and professional entertainment in Portsmouth usually took place at either the Theatre Royal in the High Street or the Green Row Rooms. The latter, which had been built in 1812, stood on the corner of Pembroke Road and St Nicholas Street. The ground floor was used as a schoolroom where Dr Bell's system of education was practiced, and the upper storey as a place of fashionable entertainment. Such widely diverse artists appeared there as the Infant Sappho, a five-year-old singer who was billed

as 'one of the most extraordinary instances of precocity on record', and Rubini, 'the greatest tenor singer in the world', on his farewell tour. But perhaps the most memorable concert was on 17 August 1840, when the pianist Franz Liszt visited Portsmouth on a provincial tour which followed a series of concerts in London. His party included Mr Mori, with whom he played a duet, and three singers, Mlle de Varny from La Scala, Miss Louisa Bassano, and John Orlando Parry, a well-known composer of comic songs who must have liked what he saw of Portsea Island, since he returned a few years later to be organist at St Jude's Church. The programme seems to have been very varied but the full extent of Liszt's contribution is not known, although he was advertised to play his own, oft-repeated *Grand Galop Chromatique*. Tickets were six shillings each or twenty-one shillings for a party of four. One would like to know the reactions of the musical Treakells and their friends to the strikingly handsome virtuoso of twenty-nine with his arrogant bearing, love of acclaim and penchant for showmanship. Sadly the *Hampshire Telegraph* was tantalizingly silent on this occasion. More interest seems to have been aroused among its staff by the arrival of Batty's Royal Circus.

The Theatre Royal, which during these years passed through a series of vicissitudes, provided very varied entertainment for the population, including a wide range of international musical talent. In 1839 an Alpine quartet dressed in Tyrolean costume sang and played their national songs; another time the American, Henry Russell, the composer of 'Woodman spare that tree', entertained with ditties 'interspersed with anecdotes of Negro life and character'; late in 1847 and early in 1848 there were concerts by the 'Ethiopian delineators', apparently a band of minstrels. In September 1848 there was a visit from the English Opera Company, which staged Donizetti's *The Daughter of the Regiment, La Somnambula*, and other musical delights. Two months later, *L'Assemblée des Sylphides* was performed by the twenty-four dancers of the Italian Opera ballet. Concerts by distinguished instrumentalists were also arranged. Raggimondi Paganini the flautist, Remy the violinist, and the Portsmouth-born harpist, J. B. Chatterton, are among the many artists who appeared there during these years. Advertised as 'a great treat' in 1843 was a concert by the theatre's own orchestra which, it was promised, 'will not only be numerous but complete in every department'. A few years earlier, in 1838, Johann Strauss the elder had come to the theatre on one of his tours. 'The execution of the

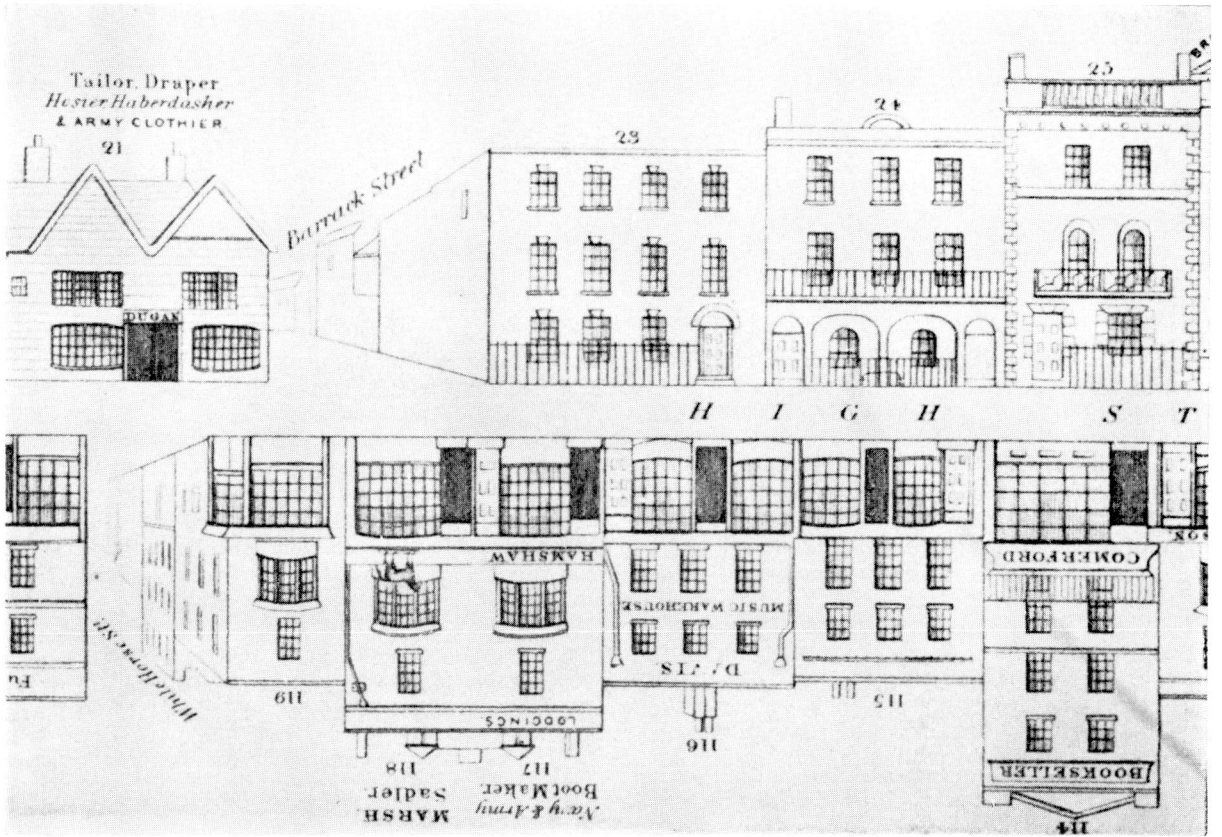

music selected fully justified the widely spread fame of this unrivalled band, which consists of no less than twenty-nine performers', the *Hampshire Telegraph* reported. 'It is impossible to convey by description any adequate idea of their exquisite performance.' Unfortunately the audience, 'although most fashionable, was not so numerous as we desired to see it'. In spite of this Strauss was prevailed upon by 'the most distinguished families in the neighbourhood' to give another concert at the Beneficial Society's Hall in Portsea, and despite a brief postponement because of a minor accident to the composer, the second performance, attended by another fashionable audience, was a triumph for the sponsors. 'The scientific performance of his most admired band,' we are told, 'throughout produced rapturous applause.'

The dramatic fare provided for the Theatre Royal's patrons was also very varied. Touring companies came regularly to present productions of popular farces, comedies and tragedies, and many distinguished actors and actresses drew large and appreciative audiences. In 1840 Charles Kean, son of the more celebrated Edmund, undertook three major Shakespearian rôles on successive nights, followed after a well earned Sunday break by another character portrayal in *The Lady of Lyons*. Eight years later the same play provided a vehicle for Fanny Kemble, who also appeared in *The School for Scandal*. In 1846 the Senegalese actor, Roscius, 'the only actor of colour that was ever known', offered his interpretation of Othello and also performed several less challenging rôles, such as that of Friday in *Robinson Crusoe*. *Sam Weller, or the Pickwickian*, was presented in March 1838, a surprisingly early dramatization of Dickens's book, which had appeared only a few months before. Soon after came a highly popular drama, *The Mutiny at the Nore*. Another nautical piece, *The Wreck of the Royal George*, which was presented in 1840, was no doubt inspired by Colonel Pasley's efforts at that time to remove the remains of the ill-fated ship by explosives, an operation which had caused considerable interest among the townspeople. At Christmas a pantomime was usually staged. Nevertheless running the theatre was an uphill struggle for the management. Despite the 'extraordinary metamorphosis' it underwent in 1844, when a refurbishing of the interior made it 'one of the most elegant theatres in the provinces', crowded houses were the exception. Too often the local newspaper was forced to bemoan a lack of interest.

The exact composition of the theatre's *clientèle* can now be little more than guessed at. On gala occasions, when well-known personalities dominated the stage, the audience was probably made up principally of high-ranking officers and their wives, and members of the local gentry. Such evenings were no doubt only made possible by their patronage. Run-of-the-mill programmes, which usually consisted of several distinct and very varied dramatic and musical items, were no doubt watched by a cross-section of the population, including many High Street residents. It is known that one night in January 1843 Mrs Parkinson of the Three Tuns was at the theatre because while she was enjoying herself her hostelry was burgled; and Henry Slight, physician and local historian, obviously enjoyed a good play, because from his pen came a drama that was performed in 1824. One section of the audience invariably consisted of young officers and their friends, who had a reputation for playing the fool. In April 1838 the *Hampshire Telegraph* drew attention to an incident at the theatre a day or two earlier. 'We cannot help intimating to a young scion of nobility,' it commented acidly, 'that it is no proof of his noble descent to take a Newfoundland dog to the stage-box . . . with a host of encouraging companions, to drink bottle after bottle of champagne, and then offer a bet "that he hits a friend on the nose with the empty bottle", seated on the opposite side of the house. Such conduct annoys and alarms females who go to be amused,' it concluded, 'and is calculated to injure the manager, in justice to whom particularly it should be thus publicly denounced.' It is unlikely that many of the ordinary Portsmouth workpeople had much chance to attend the Theatre Royal. This is borne out by an interesting editorial comment in the *Hampshire Telegraph* in September 1843. Referring to the magistrates' decision to licence a rival theatre in Landport for music only, it said: 'It appears to be saying to the poorer classes, "You low and illiterate fellows, who can only afford to swill porter and drink beer, shall not be permitted to witness the legitimate drama unless you come to our shop, the high-priced playhouse: the prohibition we extend to you is to prevent your seeing and hearing what can only be understood by the educated aristocracy".'

The newspaper was equally outspoken when it felt that the quality of a performance deserved it. It praised the production of *Pizarro* in 1839, but perfection was not achieved because of the deficiencies of one particular actor. After commenting that he was 'the only one of the *corps dramatique* without merit', it went on with brutal frankness: 'Mr Morton's Alonzo was execrable: this gentleman is never perfect in his part, an offence for which there is no excuse; nor does he possess one attribute that recommends, or ever will recommend him to the stage. The manager must last night have bitterly felt how incompetent Mr Morton is to fill any prominent character; and we trust we shall never again see him in one.'

During the mid-'forties another centre of entertainment was the Dolphin. Tickets could be bought at the bar for seats, including refreshment, in the pit (6d.) or the boxes (1s.). In June 1843 the management offered a different programme every night. Songs, bands, even a ballet were billed. Twice the magistrates refused a licence for the performance of plays, the hostelry being described as 'unfitly situate . . . too near the original theatre'. Eventually, however, perseverance triumphed over consistency, and permission was granted for a centre of dramatic activity which was known as the Royalty. Unfortunately the new theatre's life was very short. In August 1845 its interior fittings, including scenery, benches and gas chandeliers, were sold by public auction.

The early Victorians had an insatiable appetite for all kinds of entertainment, and extravagantly worded advertisements frequently appeared in the local newspaper drawing attention to the arrival of a novel exhibition or a visitor with unusual skills. Some shows were not only sources of wonder but also of educational interest. Mr Henry's 'planetarium and other extensive scenery, illustrative of universal stellar creation', accompanied by his popular astronomical exposition, had the Theatre Royal filled with enthusiastic patrons in 1847, and the same year a space of 144 square feet of a room in the old Crown Hotel was occupied by Dubourg's scale models of ancient and modern Jerusalem. Even Mr Hay the chemist, of 53 High Street, cashed in on the popular demand for knowledge spectacularly presented by conducting a series of scientific experiments on his premises, for which he charged an admission fee. Among the more memorable visitors to the town in January and again in August, 1845, was the young 'General' Tom Thumb, who held 'levees' three times a day in the Green Row Rooms, 'to gratify the curiosity of the Portsmouth folks'. On one occasion he was indisposed and medical aid was hurriedly summoned, but 'the renowned pigmy was soon himself again'.

Among the best known of the town's inhabitants were several artists. In the High Street lived, first at number 138 and later at 142, Mr James Calcott, and at number 135 Mr Ubsdell. Round the corner in Green Row were the studios of George Cole, father of the more famous Vicat, and Mr Poote. These artists painted portraits of local worthies, views of estates for their proud owners, and set pieces of memorable events, such as that of Queen Victoria meeting the Corporation in 1842, which was the work of Ubsdell. 'The portraits are all good,' it was said at the time. 'That of our chief magistrate (Daniel Howard) is perfect.' They also ran drawing and painting academies. Mr Calcott, for example, who boasted a 'bold and effective style which has given so much satisfaction', established in 1847 a class for young ladies. For a fee of a guinea a term, a pupil was taught the rudiments of perspective and sketching from nature. Drawing and painting materials were obtainable from Charpentier's Artists' Repository (no. 50), opposite the parish church. Another artist, Mr Bosanquet, who specialised in miniatures and profiles, established himself at number 102 in 1847, where he offered to provide 'the most strikingly correct likenesses . . . in various styles, from bronzed profiles at 2s. 6d. to beautifully finished coloured, from 7s. 6d. to 15s. and one guinea'. The middle class demand for competently painted family portraits continued unabated into the second half of the century, but as early as 1846 an ominous news item appeared in the *Hampshire Telegraph*. It informed the public that Mr Dowle, a photographer, was in business at 13 King Street, Portsea. According to the report he was a pioneer to whom was due the credit for introducing into England important improvements in the photographic art. When Mr Bosanquet arrived at 102 High Street, specimens of Mr Dowle's skill – 'inimitable likenesses . . . taken in a few seconds' – were already on show at number 103, across Golden Lion Lane.

No doubt on the walls of many of the High Street houses were to be found examples of the work of some of the local artists, as well as prints which had been bought from Mr Charpentier. If the residents had the means they also had the opportunity to acquire paintings of far greater quality in 1847, for two remarkable advertisements appeared in the *Hampshire Telegraph* during the course of the year. The first, in May, informed its readers of an auction to be held in early June at 76 High Street, 'by order of the proprietor, previous to the rebuilding of the premises', of 'a truly valuable collection of gallery and cabinet paintings, mostly by the old masters, in which will be found specimens of Wouvermans, Brugell, Teniers, Ostadt, Canneletti, Sconcer, Stork, Rubens, Rembrant, Van Loo, Both, Vernet, and other superior masters', as well as an assortment of *objets d'art*. In September a further auction was held at the Crown Assembly Rooms, Pembroke Road. This was of 'a superior collection of oil paintings, principally by the old masters . . . including among others . . . Murillo, Omegouck, Reinegale, Vanderpool, Halls, Droogsloot, Rembrandt, Hutenberg, Metser, Polenberg, Teniers, Ostadt, Cuyp, etc.', as well as works by Cooper, Morland, Maston, Wilkie, Wilson and Opie. 'The collection,' it was said, 'is eminently worthy the attention of connoisseurs, and the trade; the major part of this collection is in the same condition as imported, never having been in the hands of dealers.'

For those with literary interests there were the High Street bookshops and libraries in which to browse. Until 1846 number 102 was occupied by John Miller, who had a stock of about three thousand new and secondhand books for sale, as well as a circulating library of some five thousand volumes. Sophia Comerford then took over the shop, which was more commodious than number 114, where she, and before her, her late husband, had carried on business as stationers and booksellers for some years, and had also run the so-called Portsmouth Subscription Library. Both the Literary and Philosophical Institution in St Mary's Street and the Mechanics' Institution (Athenaeum) in Portsea had libraries which were available to members, and for the better-off there was the Hampshire Subscription Library in Ordnance Row, the entrance fee for which was three guineas and the annual subscription £1 3s. 6d. The Unitarian, Baptist, Independent, and Wesleyan chapels all had libraries which anyone could join irrespective of religion.

Essential to any community is a lively local newspaper. In Portsmouth the need for news and comment was admirably satisfied at this period by the *Hampshire Telegraph and Sussex Chronicle*, which was published by William Harrison at 81 High Street. At the beginning of the reign it appeared each Monday and cost fivepence, but during 1844 the day of issue was changed to Saturday, and two years later the cost rose to sixpence. Liberal in character, it frequently spoke out with great vigour on behalf of the poor and oppressed and commented fearlessly when the need arose on the follies and misdemeanours of those in authority. Reform meetings were usually given good coverage and sympathetically reported, but the Chartist movement was violently opposed. This apparent contradiction was explained by the editor in 1843. After repudiating the suggestion 'that we are changing our principles and quitting the ranks of the reformers', he wrote: 'We believe Chartism to be Republicanism . . . we glory in the name of reformers.'

The paper had a comparatively wide circulation for the time. In 1841 its average weekly sale was over 3,300 copies, making it one of the leading local newspapers in the south of England, easily outstripping the *Salisbury Journal* and the *Bristol Mercury*. At the beginning of the reign it was a simple news-sheet of four sides, rather amateurishly produced, gossipy, and frequently wildly inaccurate. In 1846 it was completely transformed. Doubled in size to eight pages, it assumed a far more professional appearance. Less parochial in outlook, it carried much more national and international news. One of the reasons for this transformation was probably increasing competition from the London papers. In the days of the stage-coach they had been slow to arrive in Portsmouth, but by early 1847, with the development of the railway, a dramatic change had occurred. The London morning newspapers could be bought at Mrs Comerford's or Garnett and Newcomb's, at the corner of the new market house, at 10.15 a.m., and evening editions arrived from the capital for sale at 8.30 p.m.

The editor of the *Hampshire Telegraph* was an enthusiastic cricket supporter, and this 'manly game', which was played on Southsea Common, was strongly recommended to the young men of the town. In 1840 he maintained that 'of all the sports practiced either al fresco or by gaslight, there is none can be placed in competition with cricket, tending as it does to infuse health and vigour into the frame, and to engender that sort of blood which we cannot but regret the lack in the billiard-playing, long-haired, cigar-smoking youth of the present day'. Although billiards was frowned upon by the local press, it had the stamp of approval of the Prince Regent, who installed a table at Osborne. The game was played by the public on several of the High Street premises, including the Dolphin, the Navy and Army Clubhouse, which Mr Parkinson of the Three Tuns opened for officers at number 95, next door to his hostelry, in 1844, and at Mr Sherwood's (no. 68), where there was also a public shooting gallery. An establishment at 6 Battery Row also had billiard rooms.

Sudden and dramatic were the fires that occasionally broke out, seriously endangering whole sections of the street if they were not quickly discovered and dealt with. In January 1845, for example, there was considerable panic when smoke was seen rising from the former Crown Hotel (nos. 34-36), which was then divided into two shops, one of which was occupied

by Mr Blackwell, an upholsterer and cabinet-maker, and the other by Mr Sargeant, fruiterer and ginger-beer manufacturer. The source of the fire was one of the furniture stores at the back across a narrow yard. A formidable fire-fighting force was soon on the scene. Consisting of the police, soldiers, neighbours, and two hundred dockyard workers, and aided by the borough, garrison, gunwharf, dockyard and Royal Marine barracks engines, it was at first power-less because of a shortage of water, 'none happening at the time to have been laid on in the pipes of the Waterworks Company'. Eventually, however, the mains were filled, 'when all hands went to work with the engines with great spirit'. The fire was confined to the back premises, but Mr Blackwell lost a con-siderable amount of stock, and although he was insured for £1,000, put his losses at double that amount. When the fire was at its height it was decided to evacuate the old Crown and the Vicarage next door. Willing hands, exercising 'great caution . . . against the slightest injury', brought out the Rev. McGhie's prized possessions and packed them in waggons. But at Mr Blackwell's the story was different. There was 'much recklessness', it was reported, 'the windows and frame-work were un-necessarily broken in, and furniture of all descriptions, including looking-glasses, etc. indiscriminately hurled from the windows of the first and second floors upon the pavement, when all might have been brought down the stairs and carried away without the slightest injury. Much loss has been sustained by this.' The undamaged stock in Mr Blackwell's shop was taken for safety to friends' houses opposite and to the churchyard. The contents of some of the dwellings in Penny Street were also hastily removed by the zealous military and shared in the general damage;

but at Messrs. Badcock and Colenutt's furniture store on the corner of Pembroke Road not an article was shifted and not a pennyworth of mischief done, owing to the cool nerve and determination of Barber, their salesman. The shortage of water caused a good deal of comment afterwards, and the suggestion from the *Hampshire Telegraph* that there should be a permanent reservoir at Pembroke Bastion. The water, it was argued, could be let out daily to cleanse the gutters in dry weather, and a new supply furnished by harnessing the treadmill power of the prisoners in the gaol, so making their exertions of practical use to the community.

Not surprisingly, the high spirits of the young men of both the town and the armed forces led to occa-sional outbursts of noisy behaviour and vandalism. As early as 1840, when new bye-laws were suggested, it was said: 'No one can have forgotten the dis-graceful outrages committed in these towns during the last and the preceding winter, in tearing down signs, wrenching knockers from doors, ringing bells, and wantonly alarming and disturbing the inhabitants at unreasonable and improper hours.' That year there was a craze for interfering with the street lighting; in 1842 culprits who were never traced ignited gun-powder on a landing at the George and caused an explosion which blew doors off their hinges, burned the carpets, shattered glass, and could be heard in the Pembroke Road police station a hundred yards away; in 1845, some 'who would feel highly insulted if they were not called gentlemen' smashed a window in Mr Emanuel's drawing-room with a detonating cracker and damaged both faces of the clock which hung outside his shop. The *Hampshire Telegraph* never missed an opportunity to castigate the authors of such misdemeanours, but when the town as a whole came in for criticism by outsiders, it was the first to spring to the defence. 'Portsmouth has an ill-name in public estimation for the behaviour and morals of its inhabitants,' it commented in January 1846, 'and most undeservedly do strangers imagine that a laxity of proper feeling predominates among its females. We who know the place', it went on, 'have ever scouted the injustice of this charge against its population.'

Once a year, however, in mid-July, the noise, the drunkenness, the immorality, and the protests of the residents reached a climax. Since medieval times the Free Mart Fair had been held in the High Street, but whereas it had once been an important centre of regional trade, by the nineteenth century it had deteriorated into a fortnight-long Saturnalia which attracted pickpockets and prostitutes, deserters and derelicts. 'It creates great dissatisfaction among the respectable inhabitants', it was stated in the detailed *Report* which preceded the 1835 Municipal Corporations Act. 'Disreputable characters of every sort haunt the town during its continuance, and the streets are in a state even more disorderly than usual. Many of the inhabitants quit Portsmouth for the time to avoid the nuisance.' By day the High Street residents looked out on the gingerbread stalls and the hucksters selling gewgaws and trinkets; by night they shuttered themselves against the crowds passing to and from the numerous sideshows on Grand Parade, and the notorious Vauxhall, a dancing tent which was open until the early morning hours. During the first Victorian decade the clamour for the fair's abolition grew stronger, and eventually success was achieved in 1847, to the intense relief of the Corporation.

Its demise helped to mark the end of an era, another significant reminder to the townspeople that all around them the world was changing dramatically. At the accession of the Queen the stage-coaches had rumbled up and down the High Street; a decade later, swiftly and surely they had gone for ever. The old mail coaches were soon forgotten and there were already complaints in 1848 about a postal service which a year or two earlier would have been considered remarkable.[18] Within an incredibly short space of time the railway engine had become an acknowledged feature of the landscape and its effects on society were daily more evident. In 1848, for example, the town council was asked to debate the need for local church clocks to keep London time, 'so as to be correspondent with the time kept at the railway station'. The same year, on the second day

of Portsdown Fair no less than 15,000 people were said to have taken advantage of the cheap excursion to Cosham from Landport Station.

With the emergence of the new half-century, the old town of Portsmouth found itself being overwhelmed more and more rapidly by the expanding suburbs. Rival shopping centres were developing apace, and new hotels like the Portland in Southsea and the Sussex in Landport were attracting an increasing number of visitors. Across the Common from the sea, the fashionable villas that were transforming the area were much more desirable to the middle class than the old houses crowded within the circuit of the ramparts. By the 1880's the combined market house and civic centre of which the early Victorian inhabitants had been so proud was neither sufficiently commodious nor convenient for the needs of a growing city, and a splendid new guildhall was built inland away from the old town. The High Street finally lost the primacy it had enjoyed for centuries.

ACKNOWLEDGEMENTS

I owe a special debt of thanks to Mrs Patricia Haskell for generously sharing with me her own detailed knowledge of the High Street and its history, and commenting on various aspects of this *Paper* while it was still in draft form. Dr D. Dymond and Mr John Alexander also made valuable criticisms at an early stage. Miss M. Butler and Miss C. Booth of the Central Library, and Miss P. Swan and Mr A. Corney of the City Museums very kindly helped me to select the illustrations, which were skilfully reproduced for publication by the City Engineer's Department. My sincere thanks are also due to Mr G. F. Tucker, Technical Adviser of the *Portsmouth Papers* series, for drawing the map of the High Street.